Top Cat Breeds

Abyssinian

Bernard Conaghan

TABLE OF CONTENTS

A Crabtree Seedlings Book

Crabtree Publishing
crabtreebooks.com

School-to-Home Support for Caregivers and Teachers

This book helps children grow by letting them practice reading. Here are a few guiding questions to help the reader with building his or her comprehension skills. Possible answers appear here in red.

Before Reading:

- What do I think this book is about?
  - *I think this book is about what Abyssinian cats look like.*
  - *I think this book is about how Abyssinians act.*
- What do I want to learn about this topic?
  - *I want to learn how Abyssinians act.*
  - *I want to know what Abyssinians look like.*

During Reading:

- I wonder why...
  - *I wonder why they have green or gold eyes.*
  - *I wonder why their coats are short or medium.*
- What have I learned so far?
  - *I have learned some Abyssinians that are one color are rare.*
  - *I have learned most Abyssinians have a ticking pattern.*

After Reading:

- What details did I learn about this topic?
  - *I learned their coats do not need brushing.*
  - *I learned Abyssinians are affectionate and loving.*
- Read the book again and look for the glossary words.
  - *I see the word* ***shed*** *on page 10 and the word* ***prey*** *on page 12. The other glossary words are found on pages 22 and 23.*

The Abyssinian is a top cat **breed**!

Its body is long and it has strong muscles.

Abyssinians have green or gold eyes.

Their **coats** are short or medium length. They feel silky and smooth.

Photo Fun Fact

There are tufts of fur in their large ears.

Abyssinians that are one color are rare.

Most Abyssinians have a pattern called **ticking**.

Their coats do not need brushing. Abyssinians **shed** very little.

Photo Fun Fact

The fur is darker on its spine.

Exercise is important. These cats love to play **prey** games.

Abyssinians are very **social** and enjoy company. They love jumping and climbing.

Fun Fact

These smart cats can be trained to do tricks!

Abyssinians are **affectionate** and loving.

They are quiet cats
with soft voices.

Abyssinians make great pets. Would you like to **adopt** this top cat breed?

Cat Adoption Quiz

Are you ready to add a cat or kitten to your home? Answer “yes” or “no” to each question.

1. I have a lot of space for a cat.
2. I will feed my cat the right foods every day.
3. I will clean the litter box every day.
4. I will play with my cat daily.
5. I am ok if my things get ruined.
6. I will provide my cat with interesting toys.
7. I will not force my cat to do things.
8. I understand that not all cats like to snuggle.
9. I understand that all kittens grow up to be cats.
10. I will make sure my cat feels safe.

How many “yes” answers do you have?

0–5: You are definitely not ready to adopt. Maybe in a year or two.

6–8: You can start talking about adoption.

9–10: You understand how to be a responsible cat caregiver. You are ready to add a cat to your family.

Cat Playtime

Do

- Make play a daily habit.
- Use wand toys to keep your cat far away so you don't get scratched.
- Make toys from cardboard boxes with entry and exit holes.
- Play with each cat separately if you have more than one cat.
- Pull the "prey" away from the cat and not towards it.

Don't

- Keep a toy in your hand and then tease your cat to get it.
- Encourage play with body parts, such as fingers.
- Place toys close to your cat's face.
- Frustrate your cat by only using laser pointers they can't catch.
- Punish a kitten or cat that scratches or bites during play.

Glossary

adopt (uh-DOPT): To take a pet home and be its caregiver

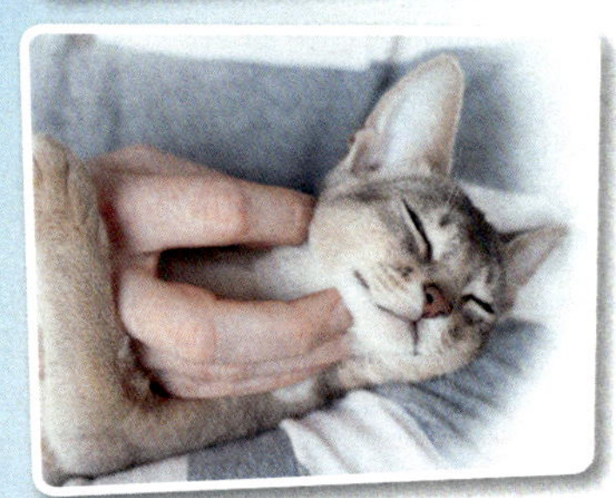

affectionate (uh-FEK-shuh-nit): Showing love

breed (breed): A particular type of animal within a group of animals

coat (koht): The natural fur or hair that covers an animal

prey (prey): An animal that another animal hunts for food

shed (shed): To cast off hair

social (SOH-shuhl): Friendly

ticking (tik-ing): A pattern of dark flecks on the tips of a cat's fur

Index

About the Author

Bernard Conaghan lives in South Carolina with a German shepherd named Duke and a black-and-white rescue cat named Duchess. He is a coach on his son's football team. He always eats one scoop of peach ice cream after dinner.

Written by: Bernard Conaghan
Designed by: Jen Bowers
Series Development: James Earley
Proofreader: Kathy Middleton
Educational Consultant: Marie Lemke M.Ed.

Photographs: Shutterstock: Cover and throughout: ©2014 Kasefoto, © Nadya_Art, © Studio Ayutaka, © Net Vector, © ANNA_KOVA; p.3 frame © Denis Cristo; p.4 ©2019 Anastasija Kru; p.5 ©2018 Alla Lla; p.6, 22 ©2012 janecat; p.7 ©2020 evrymmnt; p.8 ©2018 vilma3000; p.9, 23 © 2015 Dmitrij Skorobogatov; p.10, 23 ©2022 Savvapanf Photo; p.11 ©2016 Utekhina Anna; p.13, 23 ©2016 Seregraff; p.15 ©2019 Anastasija Kru; p.16, 22 ©2022 Nataliabiruk; p.17 ©2017 Seregraff; p.18 ©2022 Nataliabiruk

Crabtree Publishing

crabtreebooks.com 800-387-7650

Printed in Canada/012024/CP20231127

Published in Canada
Crabtree Publishing
616 Welland Ave.
St. Catharines, Ontario
L2M 5V6

Published in the United States
Crabtree Publishing
347 Fifth Ave
Suite 1402-145
New York, New York 10016

Library and Archives Canada Cataloguing in Publication
Available at the Library and Archives Canada

Library of Congress Cataloging-in-Publication Data
Available at the Library of Congress

Hardcover: 978-1-0398-3845-1
Paperback: 978-1-0398-3930-4
Ebook (pdf): 978-1-0398-4012-6
Epub: 978-1-0398-4084-3